Manna from Mama

Chimara P. Swift

Manna from Mama

Chimara P. Swift

© 2019 Pamela Smith

ISBN: 978-0-9986152-0-2

All rights reserved. Except for use in any review, the production or use of this work, in whole or in part, is forbidden without the written permission of the author.

The stories, locations, experiences and dialogues in this book all come from the author's recollection.

For permissions contact:

    chimarapswift.author@gmail.com

Printed in the United States of America.

BELLA JOHNS ENTERPRISES
PUBLISHER

Dedicated

To My Mama

Shirley Davis

1917-1996

Who Taught Me Well

Contents

Come Sunday	1
Get a Prayer Through	26
The Old Lady and Her Dog	28
First Day of School	33
Who Broke My Lamp?	44
Manna from Mama	57
Without A Song	70
About the Author	*78*

Acknowledgements

I thank God, who gave me gifts and has been so patient, loving, gracious and kind while waiting for me to open them.

To my sisters and brothers, Rommey too, who is not mentioned in *Come Sunday* because he was probably in the kitchen eating.

To my daughters, Tia and Naomi, who love me anyhow.

To my son Eian.

To Michelle, my only friend, who has listened to me and my stories for almost 50 years and has loved me wherever I was standing.

And a special thanks to my sister, Marsha, who never, never, never gave up on me (well one time, but it was a lesson in tough love).

To Dr. Ulysses Q. Chambers, my English professor at Chicago State University, who taught me how to find my voice.

And a special thanks to all my Stony Island Avenue supporters.

Foreword

It's only natural that my first project would be about my mother. Other than myself, I feel as if I know her best, and Mama was my biggest fans.

My Mother Knew How to Get a Prayer Through is a song. The music I hear is my mother's because I do not play an instrument or know anything about the mechanics of music. But I hear these complete songs in my head which I attribute to her love for music. Mama played the piano, sang around the house all the time, took us to church every Sunday, and to musical and glee club competitions, which were a lot more popular in those days.

Come Sunday is a story about a typical Sunday morning in the Smith household. I can in no way say me and my mother got along well. I was her problem child – but she did not allow me to be a problem nor did she slack in disciplining any of us. In those days, therapy, psychology and counseling were unheard of among poor families, so Mama had to teach me herself how to behave. She made me be still when she'd see that wildness in my eyes, or she'd give me a book to read or some colors or something to do.

It wasn't until recently that I got the revelation that Mama didn't know anything about bi-polar or schizophrenia, but she knew me. She knew all her children. And she knew what I needed to learn so that my life would work and I would be productive.

So, in understanding that, I have returned to the simple things she taught me to help me with my struggle with mental illness. Like in *Come Sunday*, my behavior can often come across as rebellious or disobedient. The truth is: I have trouble focusing on life because of the many voices and distractions that run through my mind, making it hard for me to concentrate.

For some strange reason, writing works for me. It is the process of building words into sentences, sentences into paragraphs, paragraphs into pages, pages into chapters, that make it a doable thing for me – I can work through the process with the patience Mama taught me. Without even realizing it, my mother had given me the tools I needed to be successful in life. I am so confident in this theory that now, after more than five decades, I am putting those tools into practice to complete this, my first book, which I've titled *Manna from Mama*.

The short story, Manna from Mama really happened. And for me, it happens often in my life where I know my mother supplies me with the thing I need to get through a day. She is there always looking after me in the things she taught me. They enrich my life, and no one can ever take them from me. They are a constant source of her love for me and they help me to survive and be creative.

Most importantly, Mama taught me about God. And she knew 'for real for real' how to get prayer through.

Included in this book you will find what I call 'Mama-isms'. These are sayings my mother would say to make important points. She never cursed, but she could 'word whip' you with these truths and reprimand you in such a way you would beat up on yourself. I always thought those Mama-isms were a little crazy, but as I grew older, they made more sense to me. I now cherish these little nuggets of wisdom.

Speaking of getting prayers through, I had no idea when I walked to the Stony Island Arts Bank in the summer of 2016 to look into the Writers Workshop that I would be publishing a book. At the Arts Bank I found the missing pieces I needed to make my dreams come to fruition.

Included in this book is an excerpt from my novel, *Without a Song*, which chronicles my life and my ten years as a breast cancer survivor. It is scheduled for publication in Fall 2020. I am excited because writing is my absolute favorite thing in life to do.

In all my joy, I can't help but shed a tear for my sisters, Pippie and Toostie who recently died. They always encouraged my writing. I wish they were here so I could tell them I finally figured it out.

I hope you enjoy these tales about me, my mother and my crazy sisters and brothers.

Mama

She looked real pretty. Her soft curly hair framed a cute freckled face that worked hard to look angry.

She didn't wear make-up or allow her girls to wear it either.

"All yous got to do is pinch your cheeks and bite your lips and put a little vanilla behind your ears. You girls are made of good stuff." She would say this with enough vanity for all of us.

Yous. She thought all she had to do was put an 's' on the end of a word to make it plural:

"Yous be ready."

Come Sunday

It was a mad house in there with Mahalia spreading a soulful calming balm as she sang "soon I will be done with the troubles of the world." It was an oxymoron in action. Mama had combed my hair out first. She had straightened all the girls' hair the evening before. My sister had rolled my bangs and my shoulder length hair with brown paper bag and put a clean pair of bloomers on my head. This was to help keep my homemade hair rollers in place, but we both knew that my hair would be a mess in the morning. There would be pieces of brown paper bag tossed everywhere, bloomers – who knows where, and my hair sticking straight up in the air. They, my other sisters, claimed this was because I was a rough sleeper, but I wasn't. But sleeping three-deep in a bed where you are the youngest you may find yourself fighting for cover and space or you'd end up hovering on the edge of the bed – cold and without blanket.

This Sunday morning Mama had me dressed and out of the way first so that I would have time to find a new scripture for testifying service.

Chimara P. Swift

"You are too old to keep saying 'Jesus wept.' That's for babies. And you been going to church and Sunday school long enough to know some bible verses, so find something new to say this morning," she said, shoving me and my bible toward the front door.

"Go sit on the porch, and don't get your clothes dirty," she added.

She had been telling me to learn a new bible verse for testifying service for weeks now and I had not done it. When my turn would come to speak I 'd just pop up like a piece of toast; say" Jesus wept" and quickly sit down. That was my habit and I was having a hard time breaking it. But my time was up. I could tell that Mama meant business and I could not put it off any longer.

I sat on the edge of the red brick porch dangling my freshly greased patent leather shoes from skinny, but impressive olive oiled legs. As I looked downward at the bible in my hand, I noticed the fold in one of my lace trimmed socks was slightly crooked. I made a metal note to straighten it out when I stand up because bending forward from the high porch ledge could be dangerous. I lifted my dress and meticulously spread my two petticoats out wide along the edge. They reminded me of the icing on Aunt Jeanette's fluffy white coconut cake. Then I neatly spread the yellow satiny fabric of my dress over them creating an exotic wingspan. I was a yellow breasted Negro; the rarest and most exquisite bird in the Woods of Engle.

My hair was neatly comb with new ribbon and wide finger rolled bangs. A light Vaseline shine created a soft glow on my face and lips as the early morning sun spotlights me. All I needed to do now was remember my lines.

Serval Saturdays before this Mama had given us all chores to do while she was out. Mine was to clean off her dresser. She handed me an oily bottle of furniture polish and a greasy rag instructing me to wipe the dresser off real good.

"Take everything off and shake out the dollies real good, then sit everything back on it nice and neat. I'm going to check when I get back," she said, "so do a good job."

I was off to a good start, but her dresser had too much stuff on it for me to be moving it all off and putting it back, so I just pushed everything toward the back and wiped around the edges real good. I wiped the Royal Crown and Murray's hair grease cans off real good and rearranged the bottles of lotions and perfumes. It looked good to me, so I wiped the front of the dresser down and put the polish and rag away with just enough time to watch a couple of cartoons before Mama got back.

When she came home and asked me had I done what she said, I quickly answered her, "Yes ma'am.

"You shook out the doilies real good?"

"Yes ma'am"

"Let me go see how it looks," she said. "I bet it looks real nice," she said heading for the stairs.

When she called me, I could tell by her tone that she was displeased.

"I thought you told me you did what I told you to do?"

"I did," I said weakly, not taking my eyes off her as I tried to figure out if she knew, or if she was trying to get me to tell on myself (another one of her tricks). I was also keeping my eyes on her hand in case she decided to knock me upside my head for lying. In the seconds I waited to see what was going to happen next, I beat myself up pretty bad and wondered why I had lied.

After a long hard stare, which probably was my last chance to come clean, she asked, "Then why is this quarter I left for you still under the dresser scarf?"

She already knew the answer and I knew I had messed up. Wow, she had left me a quarter! That would have bought me a bag of chips or a candy bar for every school day next week. But instead of having snack money I had gotten myself in trouble and would probably end up getting a whipping or punishment if not both. I didn't dare open my mouth and add to the lie. I was cold busted, so I mumbled a half truth and a weak apology. I said I was sorry for not doing a good job, but my hands got slippery from the oily polish and I was making a bigger mess and just put things back the best way I could. Man, this was so close to the truth I was starting to believe my own lie.

Surprisingly enough she acted like she believed me too, but she didn't give me the quarter which was punishment in itself. The truth was she told me what to do and I didn't do it.

Now she was telling me to learn a new scripture for service and I knew I had to do it. She was not playing with me and I was still in hot water about the dresser. Maybe I could find something about not lying and let her know I had learned my lesson and a verse.

I looked down at the bible in my hand. I had asked my married sister Elaine to help me with a verse when I visited her house the day before.

"Oh, I can teach you a scripture," she said surprising me, "and this one will be a good one to live by too."

She must have noticed the look of surprise on my face because she added, "I use to teach Sunday school, you know?"

No, I didn't know. But then I didn't know much about her anyway. She and Mama had fallen out about her running off getting married long ago. They didn't speak for years. They'd just recently worked things out and Elaine had just that year started coming back around the family.

I liked her and I really liked her helping me out by teaching me a bible verse. I remembered it good when we went over and over it just the day before. But this morning it was gone. "Now what was it?" I asked my mind. I couldn't even think of the first word and I didn't know how to find stuff in the bible where I could look it up. What was I going to do?

I was looking for where we marked it off in my bible to see if I had the first part right. I and the other kids in my Sunday school class at Normal Park Baptist Church had slaved for months learning the books of the bible. We were presented with the King James Bible once we'd recite them out loud in front of the class. So why couldn't I remember one measly bible verse? I suddenly remembered that it was in Philippians and eagerly flipped my bible open to look in that area when my eye caught the shadow of a man slipping down the stairs into Miss B's basement apartment. Then I saw Miss B poke her head out; looking left and right before pulling him in and closing the door.

I was snapped back to attention at the sound of my mother's voice calling my name.

"Pam! Pam! Are you finished with that verse yet?"

"No ma'am," I yelled back over the noise of all the stuff that was going on in the house.

"Ouch! Ouch!" I could hear one of my sisters loudly expressing her displeasure with having her hair combed. She was the only one that did that. Maybe her head was more tender than everybody else's, because she was the only one that got away with it.

"You need to hurry up," Mama called out to me. "You've had enough time to freeze hell and thaw it out."

How could she keep up with everything everybody was doing? She still had my four brothers to get ready and two more heads to comb.

I could hear the buzzing of the hair clippers which meant Mr. Dave was in the hallway cutting hair. Amidst the buzz I could hear an occasional, "Ouch! Ouch!" and "girl be still", which took on a painful rhythm all its own. I couldn't concentrate. There was too much noise coming from inside the house.

My brothers were upstairs fighting over who knows what; a tie, a shoehorn or some insignificant piece of haberdashery that made them think they looked cool on Sunday morning. My sister Pippie was verbally searching for her shoe. Her voice rose in a panicky squeak. "Anybody seen my shoe?" she asked over and over without receiving an answer from anybody. Somebody else was on the phone trying to talk above all the noise, as Mahalia and the troubles of the world faded further and further into the background.

Philippian? Philippians what? I felt like I was on to something when all of a sudden, I heard…

"Wake up everybody the morning is wasting." It was the strong baritone voice of my oldest brother, Sunny. He was coming down the street singing his slave chant over and over as he often did once he hit the block.

He smiled as he walked up and tugged at my ankles. His smile was more brilliant then the morning sun. I could tell he was in a good mood, but before I got a chance to speak to him, my neighbor, Mr. Jones, came out on his porch and hollered across the front yard.

"How about that fight last night? That young Cassius Clay just showed out! He sure surprised me!

Sunny laughed before answering, I guess it's time for you to surprise me and pay up, he said, holding his hand out toward the old man.

"I'll be right out, just give me a few minutes, I was getting dressed for church, until I heard you out here".

"I'll be right here," Sunny answered turning his face upward toward me.

"Where's Mama?" he whispered.

"She's in the front room combing hair."

"And where is 'he'?" Sunny asked with a frown.

Everyone knew that 'he' was my step-farther Mr. Dave, who recently put Sunny out of the house. I also knew that Sunny wasn't allowed to come to the house or sit on the porch anymore. And I was getting a little nervous wondering if I should to be talking to him, or if he was standing too close to the building, so I hurried up and answered him.

"He's in there," I jerked my head toward the house in a secret gesture like motion.

Sunny knew the Sunday morning routine as well as anybody else in the household even though he didn't go to church with us, he knew the drill. Mama's rule, come Sunday, was that everybody had to get up and go to somebody's church or go somewhere. She was a stickler for order and discipline when it came to getting up going to church, school or anywhere for that matter. Everyone knew to get up when she'd call their name, wash up, brush their teeth, make up their bed and get dressed before coming downstairs for breakfast. Mama had lots of rules for Monday thru Sunday and one of the reasons Sunny got put out was that he did not follow them.

"I am not going to let you kids run my house."

We'd all heard her say this a million times, but this morning I could hear her fussing all the way out on the front porch. Sunny took it as a personal sign to get back and he drifted toward my neighbor's yard and leaned against the massive oak tree that grew there.

Despite Sunny and several of my older sisters' efforts to run our new step-farther out of the house, Sunny had gotten put out instead. He should have known Mama was not going to side with him against Mr. Dave once he finally decided Sunny had to go.

"He's too much trouble. He keeps up too much mess", I heard him tell Mama one day.

Although Mama had pleaded with him to let Sunny stay, it didn't do any good.

"No! He has to go," Mr. Dave insisted, he's a grown man and it's time he took care of himself. Plus, he is bad for the younger kids," he added, "he's always stirring' them up." He went back to polishing his twelve-and-a-half oxblood Stewart McGuire's and getting his perfectly handsome self dressed for wherever he went on Sunday's—but it wasn't the church.

Just then Glen, my brother next to me in age, ran out of the house.

"Sunny! Sunny! He shouted as he jumped down the stairs and ran around the far side of the porch.

"Hey little man," Sunny smiled and extended his hand in greeting, but Glenny charged into him playfully catching him off guard.

"Did you see it? Did you see the fight? Did you?"

"Yeah man I saw it. It was 'tuff'; Cassius Clay whipped the mess out of Liston – he beat him so bad that by the sixth round Liston wouldn't even come out into the ring. That Cassius Clay is the greatest in the world. He beat the mess out of Liston, just like I said and it won me a bunch of money," he boasted.

Glen stopped playing boxing so Sunny could reach in his pocket and show off his wad. The wad of money was like a dog whistle because before I knew what was happening, my other three brothers rushed out of the house and crowded gleefully around Sunny. After a hearty round of punches, pats, man slapping and passing out money they calmed down and listened to Sunny retell the blow-by-blow, round-by-round account of the fight for the heavy weight championship of the world. Sonny Liston vs Cassius Clay.

Sunny made some amazing body movements as he jabbed at the air, he throws a sharp left, backed up and moves in dangerously with his right. A few guys from down the block join the group and listen intently as Sunny goes on and on about the fight and how he could whip both of them in street fighting, which he claimed was a lot harder than organized, practiced ring boxing.

Suddenly a silence fell over the block and Sunny froze his action and looked upward toward the house. I thought his retelling of the fight was over but as I turned to see what everyone was staring at the source of the silence became obvious. Mama and Mr. Dave were coming out of the house. If eyes could kill you, Sunny would be dead. Maybe because it was Sunday, and no one really wanted to start a fuss, Mr. Dave and Mama headed for the old grey Buick in silence.

" You guys be ready by the time Mr. Dave get back, make sure all the doors are locked and them greens are cut off. Be sure and put the dog in the back yard. Don't leave him running around these streets loose..."

The growing roar from the 10:25 train approaching the Rock Island station grew louder and louder. Drowning out what we already knew she was going to say. So instead of repeating herself after the train passed, she just took my baby sister Debbie by the hand and got in the car.

Mama needed to be at church early, plus all of us could not fit in the car at the same time so Mr. Dave usually made two trips. I picked up my bible and headed for the car just as Pippie and Marsha came out of the house. We were all ready to go but Mama needed to pick some other family up as well, so she told us to wait until the next trip.

Finally, everyone was dressed and ready for church with plenty of time to be on time. Which Mama was going to make happen "come hell or high water" as she would say. She did not like walking in church late with a bunch of kids disturbing the order of service. But more importantly, I think the reason she pushed to get us there was because she was anxious to play her piano.

Chimara P. Swift

When Mama married Mr. Dave, we moved into this old fixer upper on 69th and Harvard and Mr. Dave brought her a second-hand upright Wurlitzer, which she played often, especially when it was time for us to take a nap so she could watch her soap operas in peace. She loved that old piano even though it had a few dead keys and was in serious need of a tune up. Even now, if I close my eyes and be still inside, I can hear her singing as she played Paul Robeson's

> Without a song, the road never ends
> Without a song you ain't got a friend
> A darkie's born, oh but he's no good no how
> Without a song

I can also hear the *Bang! Bang! Bong! Bong!* of rats running through the inside of the piano playing their late-night duets and keeping everybody woke all night. It got so bad that we had to get rid of it. It was a sad day when Mr. Dave loaded that old piano up on his truck and gave it away.

Like most things in those days, through word of mouth, Mama heard about this little church which could use a piano. Since they hadn't had a piano, they needed a piano player as well. And it wasn't long after that we were going to the First Church of Gifts on 59th and State Street every Wednesday evening for choir rehearsal and every Sunday morning for church. Mama couldn't ask for a happier ending. She was so proud of her position as evangelist and pianist at that church that there was no way in the world she was going to let us kids mess it up or make her be late.

The five-hundred-pound elephant in the room that nobody dare speak of out loud was "her and all those kids" especially after Mr. Dave died. She worked hard; two and three little jobs sometimes, just so that when the caseworker would come down the street knocking on everybody's door 'Claudine style', she would skip our house. They just knew she was on welfare with all those kids, but they were wrong. Mama was proud beyond measure and one of her proudest moments was when the caseworker would come down Harvard Street and bypass our house and go to theirs.

Marsha and Pippie went back in the house but I inched closer to my neighbor's yard where Sunny was. The silence remained though, until the car turned the corner and was clear out of sight. Relief filled the air like a cool breeze on a hot muggy day once everyone realized we had escaped incident.

Since Mama was gone, I went over to where my brothers were under the tree, knowing she did not like for me to hang out where there was a lot of boys and men. I plan to listen from a respectable distance, but all of a sudden Sunny called for me to come closer. I all but ran, anxious to be invited into the circle.

"Stand right here, he ordered, placing both his hands on my shoulder and planting me firmly in an exact spot.

I looked up at him for some indication of what was happening.

"Just stand there and be still, he said and turned back to the guys. "Now let me show you exactly how it went down," he said to the growing crowd.

"Liston was tired by now, plus his eye was cut, so he never saw it coming. Cassius Clay stepped like this." He demonstrated by moving his right foot forward and swinging his body with it. That's all I remembered before

I literally saw stars. The next thing I knew I was stretched out on my bed crying.

My brothers were hovering around me with a panicked look on their faces. The first thing I heard out of their mouths was…

"Don't tell Mama. You better not tell Mama, or we'll all be in trouble."

"Tell what? What happened?" I cried.

Chucky tried to wipe away the tears that streamed down my face uncontrollably, as Sunny ordered Glenny to go get some aspirins and water. Somebody was brushing at my hair and tried to smooth my bangs back right. "Go get some ice in this washcloth." Sunny told Alan. I panicked. I thought this was some kind of make-shift surgery and began to cry louder.

"Be quiet," Sunny tried to hush me up. "You are alright, quit acting like you are about to die. It was just a little hit. If you had been still like I told you, none of this would have happened.

"Come on," he pleaded. "Please stop crying, you forgot to get your money. Where is that cute purse you got to go with those pretty shoes," he said in a soothing voice. God he was charming. And his broad beautiful smile and laughing bright eyes were hypnotizing me and calming my spirit. I was coming back and starting to remember.

"I can do …."

"No! No, don't get up just yet," Sunny said, gently pushing me back into the pillow. "Not yet just, rest a while and hold on to this," he said, as he dug deep into his front pocket and pulled out several dollar bills, pressing them firmly into my hands.

By this time Glenny was back with aspirin and water. A cold rag was pressed to my forehead covering my eyes as well, which I could tell was tight and swollen. I cringed at the icy cold touch of the compress against the sore surface above my eye. The tears started all over again.

"I'm going to tell Mama on yawl," I cried. "I'm going to tell daddy too."

"No, you ain't going to tell nobody nothing. Nobody told that you were fighting or that you took that candy from Sweety-B's," Chucky said. "So don't go blabbing cause ain't nobody blabbing on you."

I mumbled a weak, "OK."

It was hopeless. I felt trapped. I knew Mama was going to be mad at me. My uncontrollable crying turned to quiet thoughtfulness. How was I going to explain this to Mama? The last thing she'd said to me was don't go off the porch and don't get dirty. Now here I was eye swollen, hair messed up, dressed dirty and my whole body ached. As if reading my mind, Sunny began to brush at the dirt on my dress with a damp washcloth.

"Alan get that pillow and prop up under her head, he told my other brother. Sunny placed the glass of water gently in my hands and pressed two pills to my lips. I took a sip of water and almost choked on the pills. A hand quickly covered my mouth forcing me to swallow.

"There," Sunny smiled, "you'll feel better in a few minutes." Now let me finish cleaning you up so I can get out of here before 'he' gets back. Sunny got up off his knees where he was leaning next to the bed, and before I knew it, he was gone.

My brothers stared at me as if they didn't know what to do next. They were ready to abandon the project since their supervisor had left. I pushed myself upward and stumbled out of bed, my two dollars tightly clenched in my hand. Somehow I found my patent leather purse and stumbled downstairs to look for my bible.

Mr. Dave was pulling around the corner by the time I got to the porch. There was a mad dash to put the dog up, lock the door and hurry to the car to get a window seat. I crept along in silence. Before long we were piled up sitting on each other's lap and headed toward State Street.

The first thing I noticed as I limped into the tiny storefront church down on 59th Street was the larger than life painting of Jesus Christ. His outstretched bloody hands nailed to the cross made me feel as if he was being crucified again this Sunday. The crown of thorns pressed low on his brow added to my every Sunday pain of coming to that church. A tear ran down my eyes as they adjusted to the darkness and the smoke from the incense burning on the altar. The darkness of the church in contrast to the bright sunny day was depressing.

I was glad for the darkness though because Mama could not get a good look at me from where she was seated way up front at the piano on the altar. There weren't many people there. Just Mama, Mother O'Brien, the pastor and Elder Simpson and a few members. I found a chair away from my brothers and sat quietly half hearing whatever was being said.

My head hurt and certain chords Mama was banging out on the piano aggravated it further. I felt she was doing it on purpose to get my attention, but I wouldn't look up or in her direction. I was on the verge of tears again and filled with worry. How was I going to explain to Mama about my hair and dirty dress without involving my brothers?

"You better not tell Mama," the voice reminded me.

Then what was I going to tell her — I fell? Why not? I was becoming quite the liar these days, but I hadn't yet lied right there in front of Jesus Christ while he hung on the cross. I wasn't concerned so much about my dress being messed up anymore. I was more concerned with my mother's hand and what tune she would be playing on my behind. Would she get me right there in church or would she wait until I got home?

Mother O'Brien's message was long and dramatic. I couldn't begin to tell you what it was about, but from time to time she would pound her bible against the communion table to exaggerate its physical presence as a testimony to whatever she was preaching on. I was suffering silently, and no one cared. My brothers just sat there perched like little angels interested in every word she said, treating me as if I didn't exist.

Finally, it was time for testifying service and foot-washing. I listened only for the words that clued me into when it was time for the children to speak. The adults seemed to take forever. A visitor told about her eviction and how a family member had taken her and her seven kids into their home. Finally, it was time for the children. My brothers said their verses loud and clear, which got Mama's approval. I could tell by the constant nodding of her head. A few other kids struggled through theirs and before I knew it, it was my turn.

I don't know what came over me, but words began to flow freely from my mouth. I told the whole thing knowing that my brothers and my mother were going to be mad at me. But I didn't care anymore. It was all too much for me to bear. And I let the church know that whatever happened I could deal with it because Philippians 2:5 tells me that "I can do all things through Jesus Christ who strengthens me."

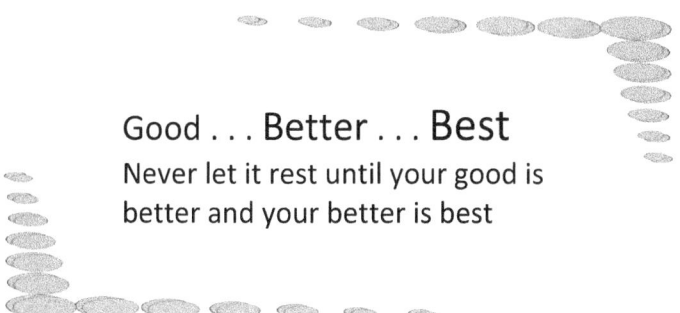

Good . . . Better . . . Best
Never let it rest until your good is better and your better is best

Chimara P. Swift

Get a Prayer Through

If you listen in the stillness of the
    early morning dawn
You can hear her as she humbly
    marches up to the throne
With power and authority
    she'd call Him out by name
She'd say, Jesus – I need to talk
    to You right away

My mother knew how to get a prayer through
She knew God personally, and she knew what to do
Sometimes, she'd approach the throne, so humble
At other times she'd be, like thunder
Claiming, in Your Word Lord, this is what You said You'd do

She'd rise at 5 o'clock in the morning
    read her Bible and say her prayers
You can hear her talking to God
    as if He was sitting right there
Her routine was Word and coffee
    whether life was good or bad
She'd always give Him praise
    and thank God for what we had

Well, now Mama, she's gone
    but I know her prayers linger on…
Cause my life is such a mess

Manna from Mama

    but I know that God is with me
I believe that in those days
    she asked Him to help me along the way
Until I learned for myself
    how to pray

(She tried to teach me)

She said, get Jesus on the mainline
    call Him up, tell Him what you want
If you knock, it shall be opened
    cause His sheep they know His voice
You know you have not
    cause you ask not
But when you ask
    ask in Jesus' name

My mother knew how to get a prayer through
My mother knew how to get a prayer through

I'd hear her pray
    she'd say Lord! Oh Lord!
She'd say I don't know
    what I'm going to do
By the time she'd get up off her knees
    the telephone would ring
And the answer to her prayer
    would be coming through

My mother knew how to get a prayer through

Chimara P. Swift

The Old Lady and Her Dog

My mother was a great storyteller. She knew some famous stories like *Why Cats and Dogs Don't Get Along, The Tale of The Wind Battling the Sun, to see which on*e would make the gentlemen shed his fleece first. I remember the gist of them and the popular ones like Aesop's fables, Mother Goose and the Bible stories she would tell us. But some of the favorites I forgot. I guess I didn't tell them enough. But here's one I love but can't remember. I know the gist of it, so I have rewritten it to an urban folk tale, with the cadence of the story which I do remember. So, here is the gist of the story called *The Old Lady and Her Dog.*

The old lady was coming home from a festival one night when she ran into a roadblock the city had put up while she gone. She had taken that road there, but it was closed now. The detour would take her six blocks out the way, because there was a railroad track and she didn't want to take that route, because it was too dangerous. She was much too tired for that, and her feet was hurting, and she was exhausted.

She saw a little low part of the roadblock and figured she could climb over it, if she was careful and took her shoes off so she could be sure-footed. Taking her time, she hung her bags over the fence, put her shoes and laid her wool sweater over the gate to avoid scratching them and began climbing. It was slow, but it was successful, and the old lady was feeling kind of good. She hadn't done anything like that in quite some time and was feeling young and spirited.

She put her shoes back on, which she had tossed over the fence, and put her sweater back on and gathered her bags. But when she commanded her dog to jump over the fence so they could continue their journey home, the dog refused. He just laid on the patch of grass near the fence.

"I know you haven't done this in quite some time either," she spoke to him, "but it aint that hard. Come on get up."

But the dog just laid there. She looked questioning at him to see if he might be sick. After all, he had eaten everything that fell to the ground during the festival, even ice cream.

"Come, come, jump over the fence so we can get home and get some sulfur to fix it."

But his facial expression was not sickness. It was how he looked when he was relaxing by the couch. He wanted to relax in the patches of grass he was resting on and ignored her.

"Oh no you don't get lazy on me. I climbed over that fence, so get your behind up."

She thought about climbing back over there and then climbing back again to go home, which killed her feeling of being young-spirited.

She commanded him several times, but he didn't move. She pleaded hopelessly and tried to bargain with him for a nice bone from the turkey leg she had brought, but he closed his eyes. She felt hopeless and didn't know what to do.

Just then she noticed a young man on the other side of the fence and asked him to help her.

"Give me a hand, young man," she said. "The dog won't jump over the fence and I cannot get home tonight."

The young man was shocked and said, "I am not feeling this, cause I need my hands, they're holding up my pants. I'm sorry old lady, but I can't lend a hand."

It was then that she spotted a piece of rope that was left at the construction site and commanded, "Rope, rope, tie the boy's pants, so he can lend a helpful hand, to spank the dog, so the dog can jump over the fence, so I can get home tonight."

But the rope refused saying, "I can't mess with a designer dude. This rope is unfashionable and can't be used."

The old lady was getting frustrated when she noticed a girl getting on the bus who had tossed her cigarette away. So, she asked the fire, "Fire, burn rope. Rope won't tie pants, boy won't beat dog, dog won't jump over the fence, and I cannot get home tonight."

He just laid there smoking slowly. Then gradually said, "I'm a smoker, not a fire. If you need a light, you got to come here to me to touch my tip. But if you need some fire, buy a lighter."

The old woman couldn't seem to get help from anybody and thought she'd climb back over the fence and take the detour cause the dog wouldn't jump over the fence being lazy. He was sleeping now. He was stretched out on the other side of the fence in the grass. No one was paying her any attention, especially not the little boy who had gotten off the bus and was busy stomping his feet in the puddle of water enjoying the splashing. He stomped one puddle so hard that the cigarette flew and touched rope.

Rope twisted and turned in a snake-like motion and caught onto boy's pants, which started a fire. Boy grabbed a switch with leaves to put it out, but in his panic, he hit the dog. The dog jumped fearful awoke and jumped over the fence, and the dog and the old lady continued on their journey home that night.

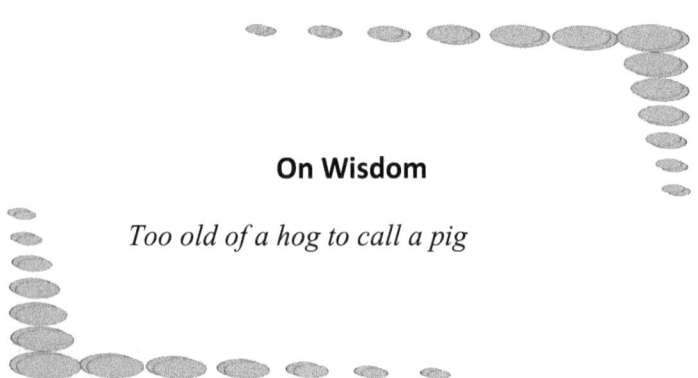

On Wisdom

Too old of a hog to call a pig

First Day of School

"I remember the day I was born…"

"Hush child, Mama commanded me gently."

"I do," I insisted. "I remember the day God made me and you pushed me out your stomach."

"Hush," Mama said more sternly as she grabbed my hand and pulled me into a pace too fast for my five-year-old bony legs to keep up without jogging or skipping.

She seemed angry and I didn't know why. I needed to finish. I was trying to tell her something important and I didn't know how.

"I do remember," I said one final time—hurt that she didn't want to her my special story about us.

"You don't know what you're talkin' about. Hush now! Hush!" She ordered me to hush, whispering almost secretly.

And I knew not to mention it to her again, but I didn't know why. So I kept my story to myself. I kept a lot of my life stories to myself. But I can't hold them anymore. I must tell somebody...

"I remember. I do."

I remember the day I was born. I remember the instant my flesh kissed the first cold blue-grey Chicago morning. I remember when my spirit, my soul, my mind merged and pushed into icy January cold from the warm comfort of my mother's womb. I wailed furiously like a whining hurricane. My life instantly felt real as God created purpose into my flesh like lightening. He told me who I was, and with the quickness as His Spirit burned in the mind like the blazing sun, I cried with fear and amazement as I entered this strange world.

"Hush child, hush," I hear Mama telling me. I am afraid to think my thought, but my mind can't be quiet. And my mother is no longer here to hush me.

My stories of who I am rage like a tempest storm upon a trouble sea. It's the big fish story that grows bigger and bigger every time I tell it. It grows from the years of my youth, my adulthood and old age. Like the catch of the day there is always something added or subtracted. It's never the same, but it is the same story. Seasoned with my life's pleasures and pains. It's my dreams, victories and disappointments.

I must make some sense of my life so God and those who touch me will understand and not judge me unfairly. I need for my children and their children to make some generational changes and hopefully live their lives with the strength and wisdom I lacked from generations of curses. I need to change the course of tides that wash life's true meaning and love away into the darkness of the sea; I need for my journey to matter and the spoils of war to be useful. I need some peace of mind. I need to rest in the comfort of my mother's arms and see home again and know my life was not lived in vain—that my life matters.

I wanted to turn back to the warmth of the house. It was my first day of school and Mama had me bundled up with so many layers of clothes I could hardly walk. We crossed Sixty-ninth Street on Harvard to an open lot, and the ferocious wind pushed me faster than I was able to move. I fall. But I raise my head, I see the school in my snowy confused vision. Parker Elementary with its ice-covered greenhouse loom over me like a massive iceberg.

Chimara P. Swift

I had looked forward to this day so long that the still cold monstrous structure looked like heaven. I was overjoyed and jumped up out of my winter grave and began to run with the wind. I could hear my mother call to me, but I couldn't stop myself. My dream of going to school was carefreely toward the stained wooden double doors of Parker Elementary School.

I met my new teacher and Mama came into the classroom with me. The first thing I saw was everyone was white. Where is Juanita the girl I talked to that was starting kindergarten, too. She invited me to her party when her grandmother was talking to Mama at the school. Where was she?

This was strange. A lot of the kids were in chairs with wheels. Two of them lay helplessly on small folding beds. There were kids with unusually large heads and wide eyes. Drool slivered down the corner of their mouths. I clung to Mama's coat. Mama's instincts must have informed her that I had changed my mind and didn't want to stay here. Mama reached down and tried to loosen my tight grip on her hand. I held on tightly and began to cry.

"Don't leave me, please don't leave. Please Mama! Please!"

I begged as she struggled to pull my hand away from her coat. I wouldn't let go. Tears rained from my eyes like a thunderstorm. Mama gave me her most serious 'you-better-stop-this-nonsense-right-now' look, but I couldn't. Neither me nor Mama could believe I was acting like this when I had been talking about going to school for months. I couldn't help it, I was consumed with fear and determined not to let go.

By this time several on my new classmates were inching up and surrounding me. The one with the mongoloid head and black empty eyes was pointing at me and staring. His eye reminded me of the deadly dark double barrels of Mama's shotgun. This is the worst nightmare I'd ever had, I thought. Why wasn't I waking up?

"Mama save me," I screamed as loud as I could. But it was too late. The skeletal one, with the long boney fingers in her mouth, pulled three juicy fingers out of her face and reached to touch me. A string of slimy saliva threaded through her fingers like a needle to thread. I screamed louder in terror as the cold white wetness pinched into my flesh. I thought she was sewing us together. A small speck of blood appeared and trickled down my smooth brown skin. I reached out and grabbed her wrist. All I could think of was the life size Raggedy Ann doll with the rubber bands on her hands and feet that Mama had brought me that Christmas. I loved that doll because I could do anything to her body and she wouldn't get broken into pieces. I could wrap her feet around my head, throw her across the room, hang her by the neck with the noose my by brother Glenny had made for me.

Before I could decide exactly what I was going to do to my new bony classmate, I was pulled into the hallway along with Mama.

"She can't stay here unless she behaves," the white women screamed at my Mama.

"Don't worry," Mama answered assuredly, "let me talk to her."

The teacher rushed back to the classroom, which by this time was in an uproar.

Mama put one hand on each of my shoulders and commanded me to be still. "Look here," she said, "white folks don't want you in their schools. White folks always looking for a reason to keep everything for them self."

She shook me slightly as she spoke now with more persistence, "Child yous smart. Just stay here and learn everything you can. This the only way you can make life better. Get you some learning in your head and don't give these white folks no reason to start takin' stuff back from you."

Our eyes were locked. She was telling me stuff I didn't understand. Uncontrollable tears ran down my face, but I did not blink or turn away. Something my mother was telling me frightened me. I could see that I did understand. All I could I think of was "hush child hush."

"Straighten up!" she commanded. "Get yourself together. Come on now. It's just for a little while and then Chuckey and Glenny will come and pick you up. You wait right there at the door." She pointed toward the exit, "And don't leave. They be here and I'm going to have you some hot chocolate ready for you when you get home.

Don't forget you gloves. Button yourself up and be sure to wrap your scarf around your neck good and tight."

She was marching me back to the classroom and I noticed each instruction took me deeper and deeper into the room. "Be good. They going to teach you how to do some of them things you always talking about in them stories you make up. Get you a good education." She leaned over and whispered in my ear as if education was some sort of special secret. "That how you get the stuff in this world. You don't want to be scrubbing floors and cleaning white folks houses all your life."

I looked at my wild-hair teacher and the kids crowded around her desk. I knew I would have nothing to do with them ever in life if it was left up to me.

"Go on now," Mama nudged me. "Make up a nice story so you can tell it to me when you get home. Gone child, this your first day of school. Quit cryin'. Yous going to be alright. Go on now." She nudged me forward as she inched back a step. "Go on!" She moved further away. Now with a sweeping hand motion she backed away, "go on now, go sit down."

I could hear her voice moving farther from me. By the time I wiped the tears from my eyes and held my head up she was gone. This was the first time in my life that my mother had left me with strangers. There was no one or nothing in the room that was comfortable or familiar this time. None of my sisters and brothers were around. My heart cried. I felt angry and alone as I cried uncontrollably. I tried to make up a story so I could tell them how I felt. I must have cried myself to sleep and when I woke up, I was all wet. As a matter of fact, it was the warm stream of liquid in my face the forced me to open my eyes. It took me a while to understand where I was what was happening because the burning spray of the liquid in my face was painful. I could hear them laughing so I took the hem of my new dress and use the scratchy wool fabric to wipe my eyes.

When my eyes were somewhat clear I looked up to see my new classmates holding little flaming pink wee wees as they pissed on me with hateful looks in their eyes. The little girls stood around watching, laughing and spitting.

"Niggar go!" The one in the wheelchair struggled to speak. "Go!"

And my new big-headed classmate sewed another slimy stitch.

That was 1957—three years after *Brown vs Board of Education* where the Supreme Court overturned the discriminatory separate but equal doctrine that further oppressed the Negro race. We weren't Black yet. We were just a few steps from slavery, especially in the South where segregation ran rampant and Negroes used separate public facilities like water fountains and bathrooms. They were not allowed in white-owned restaurants and anywhere else white folks didn't want them. We had to sit in the back of the bus and take a back seat to life.

Most of the people in the city were domestics or factory workers living in overcrowded neighborhoods, where several families dwelled in one tiny apartment. I thought life was good because we had just moved into a five-bedroom house in Englewood. We were the fourth Black family to reside in an area located south of Sixty-ninth Street. The other families were the Suttons, the

Alexanders and the Conways. Juanita Conway and I became good friends. She was in the same kindergarten room with me, but I really didn't notice that first day. But she was there with me every day until we graduated to high school.

We weren't separated, but we weren't equal that first day of school in the retarded room. The Chicago Public School system, like so many school jurisdictions, tried to subvert the Supreme Court ruling.

They did not succeed for long.

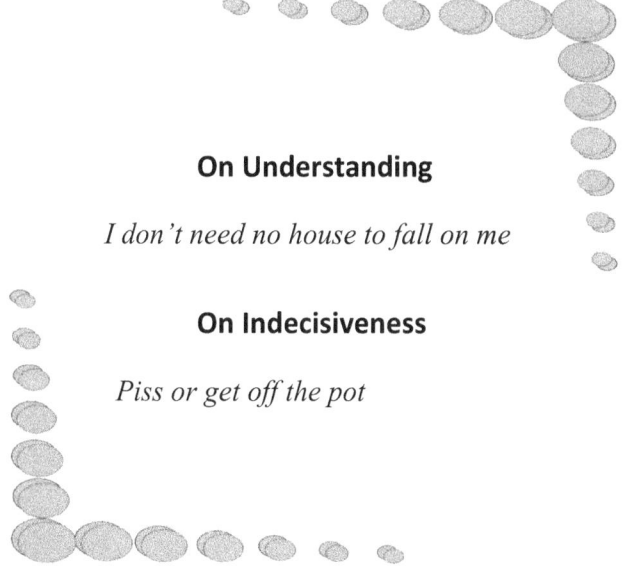

On Understanding

I don't need no house to fall on me

On Indecisiveness

Piss or get off the pot

Chimara P. Swift

WHO BROKE MY LAMP?

"Who broke my lamp?"

That was the first thing mama said when she came through the door, with groceries still in her hand, "Who broke my lamp?"

She was still in the hallway. That lamp was in the living room. How did she do that? She said she had eyes in the back of her head, but it was evident she had all kind of eyes around her. She'll be sitting in the living room and tell what you drop in the kitchen, or some stuff you just drop in the bathroom, as if she was there. The huge dining room did not buffer any sound when it came to her hearing. Even upstairs she always knew what you were getting into.

"Who broke my lamp?"

"It's not broken."

"What lamp?"

A few of my siblings chimed in unnecessarily. This was going to be a rough one, something is going to hit the fan. This was Mama's favorite lamp. Perched there on her end table, with ruffle doilies she had gotten made for it. A white woman, from Evanston, she worked for had given it to her cause she was decorating her house. Mr. Dave had to drive to get it cause she couldn't bring it on the bus.

"This lamp is from Marshall Fields and possibly an antique. Because it belong to someone else in the family before she got it," Mama had told us.

That's how black folks were in those day. They would get something somebody gave them and it was a treasure. The lamp was a delicate porcelain, with hand-painted flowers around the base and neck, with a satin shade that had a thousand fringes around its border.

"What are you waiting for! Go get those groceries, cause Mr. Dave got to get back to the barber shop."

We all scatter to go get the groceries.

"Don't put them up either, so you can get back in here cause I want to know who broke my lamp." She went into the living room. She was finally able to look at it close up. "Ump, ump ump. Can't leave these kids a minute. I could tell something was wrong when I came in here. It's turned around and that sun light reflection show off the break, I can't believe this."

Now Mama didn't do a lot of explaining and she never cursed. But she can word-whip you with finesse, make you feel real bad. When she did explain, it was to provide a clue that whoever did should confess. But no one said a word. We were all in fear, because somebody was delaying getting his or her tail whip.

Pippie broke the silence. "I was in the kitchen doing dishes and straightening out the cabinet. I was still cleaning up when you came," she said, "I didn't do it."

She had given us Saturday chores before she left shopping. Now everybody was explaining what they were doing.

Diane said she was cleaning the girls' bedroom and she just brought the garbage down to empty it.

"I help Diane with the room too, and straighten the hall dresser, and closet," I said.

"I have the bathroom and sweeping the halls and stairs," Marsha remarked.

Chucky had the boys' room, Alan had something to do in the basement and Glen had to sweep the porches and empty the trash when we got through. But there was no telling where Rommey was at cause he left right behind Mama.

"Who turn that TV on?"

Chucky answered, "I did, for Debbie."

Good answer, I thought. Debbie was the baby and didn't do nothing.

Mama took her coat off and finally said, "Hang this up somebody."

We all got up.

"It don't take but one," she said.

There was a silent pause. Mama was looking at us individually like she could tell by our face who was guilty and had done it. Mama was acting kinda strange, she was too calm for herself. It was scaring me. It was scaring all of us. All the joking had stopped. No singing our favorite song and talking about which boys and girls we like. It was serious like a family meeting. But Mama was the only one at meeting who was in the family. We were outside because she thought we had turned against her, we were hiding the truth, acting out a conspiracy to get over on her.

That old lion was going through the forest. That what she said when that Leo was going to run rampant; defending her territory.

"Glenny get me some water, would you."

Oh no. If she follow him in the kitchen, then that does it. Glenny would tell everything on us, whether it had anything to do with the lamp or not.

"I, I, I... just can't lie to Mama," he'd stuttered to me Tuesday.

"When Mama asked you was I fighting, then tell the truth that you didn't see me fighting, cause you didn't. But no, you went ahead and said I was fighting. But when Mama ask you did you clean up the yard, you said 'yes'. That was a lie, cause you just pick up two pieces of paper. And if Mama have caught you, then you'll say that you did clean it up but the wind blew it back over there, which is another lie. So, you do know how to lie, brother."

But she didn't follow him in kitchen. Instead she start to gather up the belts, of which she had several, and a razor strap, a whip and a shotgun.

"I'm going ask you one more time, who broke my lamp and if no one confess, I going to whip all of you. So, who broke my lamp?"

No one said anything.

"The person who did this need to 'fess up. Take your whipping," someone said.

"Mama I didn't do it, I didn't do it," somebody else said.

The begging and pleading had started.

"Line up," Mama commanded.

Glenny was standing there holding the water, we know he didn't do it.

While thinking of where I'll get in line, I remember I had been to the front, thinking she was going to breeze by me so she could get to the others. That didn't work. Then I went to the back, thinking she would be tired, that really didn't work. She caught her second wind and was busy to the end.

"Mama wait, wait I got use the bathroom."

Mama wasn't listening. I started for the middle of the line.

"What about Rommey? Maybe he broke it," someone said.

"That boy left here soon as I left. I saw him when he came out the hardware store." She grab the first one. "I get him when he get back here. You mind your business."

Now I am not going to tell you about my siblings' personal business, because they are going to deny it always. And some of them are not here to deny it. And whether people cry, scream bloody murder, call on Jesus, run or whatever you do while getting a whipping is personal. You don't want anybody to know it.

The stronger usually go first to get it over with, and usually don't cry. But I think when you get a whipping it's rude when you don't cry. Seem disrespectful. I'm crying before she get to me. To quote her, "I don't need no house to fall on me." Maybe she'll think I've suffered enough when she get to me.

Debbie was on the couch crying.

"Quit crying or I'll give you something to cry about."

She was in the zone on this third whipping. She was talking now. "You guys go to bed until you tell me who broke my lamp."

The two, who got theirs already ran upstairs, anxious to be out of it.

I was getting close. I felt the hits from the person she was whipping.

Oh Jesus!

She was talking about all kind of stuff: "You can forget about going to the show tomorrow. I'm not spending a dime on you guys. No Riverview, no roller skating, nothing until you learn how to live in this house without breaking something, arguing, not doing homework and cutting on that TV every time I leave this house. When you rest up, I got some more work for you. You kids done torn your drawers with me."

"Lord have mercy! I didn't do it, I swear! Oh Oh!"

"Start putting the groceries up. Get the can goods and rice."

On to the next one, not missing a beat. Then it was my turn.

"I'm not cooking yous nothing. Nothing!"

"Ah, ah, ah, ah…ah…ah…no I didn't do it. I didn't… ah…"

She was ending that one and it was me, me, me… I was stuck on me.

Sunny just popped up out of nowhere. Unless I was too busy to notice him. That is my older brother. He had all kind of ways of getting into the house. The basement, climb the balcony to the girls' room, the back door, the coal bin, or just come through the window if it was warm. He and Mr. Dave didn't get along. Mostly because Mr. Dave wanted to cut Sunny's hair. Mr. Dave was a master barber and hair was everything. Sunny had spent six months in New York (so he said) and had seen Malcolm.

"Who is that," Mr. Dave had asked.

"He's a Muslim and got an Afro hairstyle. I like it, so I'm wearing an Afro too," he said proudly.

"Well if you're going to stay in this house, you're going to cut that hair."

So Sunny was avoiding him and came by when he was gone or sneak into the house.

"Mama, what are you doing?" Sunny asked

I don't know who answered, because the next person she reached for was me.

"Somebody broke Mama's lamp."

Mama's belt was in the air... and she reaching for me.

"I broke it," Sunny said. "That's what I came back to tell you. I put some glue on it."

Mama was frozen.

"I was by early this morning. I needed my boots in the hallway for work, the boot hit it and cracked it."

Mama's hand was suspended in the air, but the belt fell limp.

"What did you say?"

He said the right thing for me. I escaped out of Mama's relaxed hand, with the quickness, to the far side of the dinner room and said a kid prayer, "Thank you, Jesus."

"I thought these kids did it and was giving them all a whipping, cause I thought they was covering for somebody or knock it down playing in the front room."

All of a sudden there, is much too much chatter in the room—Mama, us and Sunny talking all at once.

Mama started hitting Sunny, and he was twenty-five. I reckon she'll always whip us.

He started to explain, "I came to tell you, it just crack, it's not broken, but I'll get you another one."

Alan had come to the top of the stairs to listen.

"You can't get another one, that was……."

He cut her off, "You were whipping all the kids for…"

Mama cut Sunny off. "Don't question me, they did something anyway. Sitting here watching TV and not cleaning house, on the phone and everything they can get away with when I gone."

I'm going to check your work, and I bet you ain't halfway done it," she told us. And you don't come to this house unless you knock on the door and I let you in," she told Sunny.

"You doggone kids are running me wild, and you are a grown man," she said to Sunny. "But I will say I am sorry. You that got whippings can come down and watch TV. You kids that didn't get them can do housework. When I put the grocery up, I'll fix hamburgers. And Sunny, you get out."

So the kids that got whippings watched TV, did no more housework, and stayed up late. Us that didn't, finished cleaning up, did the dishes, and went to bed at bedtime. But the Smith kids did have a secret conspiracy, which was how to get even with Sunny.

And Mama, years later, when they barred parents from whipping their children said, "Well, I just have to go to jail."

On Truth

You don't believe fat meat is greasy

Manna from Mama

The bright multi-colored turkeys suspended strategically from the ceiling of the Food 4 Less, their paper machete tails fanned wide, was my first clue that the Thanksgiving holiday was approaching. The brilliant orange and gold of the cardboard horns-of-plenty, the massive squash and pumpkins, spinning in the gentle breeze of the fans, choreographed into an overwhelming presentation to showcase the holiday's special and traditional foods. It was a shopper's paradise with sampling galore.

But for me it was the beginning of massive depression. Ever since Mama died, I hated holidays especially Thanksgiving. I thought Christmas was going to be the hardest time for me, but that first Thanksgiving after Mama died caught me off guard. My grief was so intense, I drank and used so much that it was way past the New Year before I came out of it, so I never knew when Christmas came and went. This behavior became *my* tradition.

Chimara P. Swift

My mind twisted and turned like a kite in the Chicago wind as I struggled with all my being to focus on what I had come to the store to get. All was lost; I got nothing. All I could think of was Thanksgiving as my spirit slowly down spiraled into an emotional nosedive of depression. I wanted to cry but I couldn't and wouldn't. I hadn't cried in the four years since my mother died. My heart was stone; my life was filled with broken glass and cardboard boxes. I never slept. I only passed-out. I was just starting to see some light in my life, but the cornucopia of Thanksgiving paraphernalia was pricking, poking and cutting my soul, it hurt like the tears I was unable to release.

I could smell the early morning fixings of my mother's holiday meal strong in my nostrils. The sage, parsley and thyme all hovering around the pungent aroma of fresh poultry cooking with fresh diced green pepper, onions and celery sneaking up in the background like the Pips in a classic Gladys Knight song.

The memory leads me down the stairs of my mother's house and into the kitchen. As I slowly move down the aisle of the grocery store filled with flour, sugar, cake mix, icing and spices, I see her hands rolling dough as she hums a hymn. Her skilled hands flip the dough into a pie pan with ease as she sculpts the edge of the crust by pinching her fingers together.

"I must snap out of this," I say out loud – there's no way I'm going to torment myself with these kind of memories over the next 10 or 12 days leading up to Thanksgiving. My manic-depressive, schizophrenic-effective, crack behavior would surely land me in jail, hospital or an institution. It never failed. I was tired of that as well. I desperately needed to do something different this holiday season to save me the additional grief.

I don't know how or when the idea formulated. For some reason I started shopping, again—actually putting stuff in my basket that kept well without refrigeration or needing to be cooked. I love junk food anyway and I completely abandoned my plan to surprise my boyfriend with a decent meal (at his place because I was homeless). I returned to my potato chips, tuna, peanut butter, crackers, candy, and Kool-Aid street diet. I loaded up, buying twice as much food as I usually do. I had a plan and by the time I finished shopping I knew what it was.

It was a simple plan: isolation and intoxication. I wasn't even going to do the holiday. I wasn't going to be a part of the hoopla, card sending, holiday cheer, handouts or special services going on around skid row. I was going to build me a cardboard condo off the beaten path of Well-wishing Pedestrian Christian. After shopping I found the perfect box and ideal spot just off Sixth and Towne under an overgrown tree near an abandoned building. Its branches hung so low it almost concealed my cardboard box from the street.

I stockpiled water, alcohol, blankets, boxes, candles, cigarettes, drugs, matches, a glass and whatever I thought I needed for the next two weeks. It took several days for me to put everything in place and slip away from the crowd on Fifth and Crocker. But before long, I was cozy in my new place with plenty to drink and a ton of rocks to get high on. I was exhausted. I had worked hard hustlin', stealin', twistin', dealin' and doing everything I could to get money. It wasn't long before I was burning the candle at both ends, reading everything, from the

Bible (which I read every morning before I got high) to *Essence Magazine, Downtown News* and the *Los Angeles Times*. I wrote a few sad songs and letters to my daughters which I knew I would never mail. I only stepped out on occasion to see if it was day or night and to use the bathroom.

The days turned into weeks. I was lost in my own self-created darkness. I was running out of everything and didn't care. I slept more and read less. I ate very little and didn't care if it was day or night anymore. I was content in my nothingness and drifted like a lost soul at sea. I knew I was going too far but I seemed unable to stop myself. I was growing weak and I was unclear on how to get out of the box. In the days I had been inside things had shifted. I tried to find a slit or opening but seemed unable to do so. I didn't panic because nothing mattered. I found a place where there was no pain, no hurtful memories, no disappointments or loneliness, no missing my children and family, no success or failure, no nothing. I didn't even know where I was and I didn't care. I hadn't thought about the holidays or anything. I'd just drink until I passed out, wake up and drink again. I was oblivious.

That's why I didn't respond or clearly perceive the knocking sound when I first heard it. It sounded distant but the vibration of the box clued me into the realization that someone was knocking at my door. I decided to answer only because it would direct me on how to get out of the box if I should ever need to.

"Hello. Hello."

I heard what sounded like a friendly voice. I hesitated briefly before answering because it obviously was one of my party friends and I wasn't really in a socializing mood. But they were persistent, I was unable to reach the door, so I called out for them to feel free to pull up the blankets or panels or whatever (I had literally forgotten how I structured my cardboard house) and come in.

After a noisy shift with constant chattering in the background a brilliant beam of sunlight and fresh air rushed into my box and a woman's face vaguely appeared, still jabbering away, "I had two of these Thanksgiving dinners left from feeding people around the corner and I thought that maybe you would like one." She smiled as she handed me a large dish wrapped in foil.

"Happy Thanksgiving Miss," she said cheerfully.

"No thanks," I answered, "I'm not hungry." I snapped and pushed a shaky hand out in rejection of the meal. All the preparation I had gone through to make sure I didn't have to deal with Thanksgiving and here she comes. I couldn't believe this was happening. I tried to get rid of her as quickly as possible, asking her to please pull back the board for me, but she continued talking.

"This is a wonderful meal – you may not want it now but you'll surely want it later. I'll just sit it up here on the roof of your house where the sun can keep it nice and warm. Try and eat something; it will make you feel Better," she said as she left without closing the flap back down.

I was really upset now. An unnecessary interruption but I might as well use the bathroom and check on my house since the door was open. I stepped out into the bright sunlight. It burned my eyes and blinded me. Before I could focus good a car pulled up to the curb and a lady's kind and gentle voice said, "Happy Thanksgiving – Jesus loves you."

Oh this is just too much, I thought.

"Would you like some fruit?" she asked as she stuck a jeweled arm out of the window.

"No thank you!" I snapped again, groaning in aggravation.

"Here," she insisted, "you may want to eat it later. It's just some fruit and nuts. I wish I had more to give. It must be hard being homeless, especially this time of year."

I reached for the bag – almost snatching it from her hand – so she could shut-up and get on out of my way. Although I was all hurt and mean inside, I mumbled a weak "thank you" like my mother had taught me to do. I opened the bag and with that came a flood of Thanksgiving memories I could no longer avoid.

The snack was scarce, but it was the exact combination of fruit and a few walnuts and pecans with peppermints that my mother had issued to my thirteen siblings and me for many years during our childhood. There was one apple, two oranges and an old fashion game like you find in the Cracker Jack box. I sat on my crate next to my condo and tinkered at getting the little bead size ball into the eyes and nose of the face of the clown. I was determined and it took far more time and patience than it should have for an adult. My mother used to buy them for me as a child and I was always a lot quicker working them out.

I gave up once saying, "They don't make them like they used to." But I ended up picking it back up almost as fast as I put it down. It took some time but I finally got all the beads in the grooves of the clown's face which made the clown look more alive. As I placed it carefully on the roof of my cardboard condo, I noticed the dinner the strange lady had brought by earlier. I realized I was hungry and since I was up, why not enjoy a little fresh air and something to eat. Some strange impulse had me cover my crate with a flowered scarf I sometimes wore with my solid colored dresses. I was thirsty as well and I rambled around the condo until I found the one glass I owned. I washed it and filled it with water. I sat in the doorway of my house and pulled the crate with the dinner on it in front of me. I removed the foil as carefully as it seemed to have been wrapped. My enthusiasm was rising; I could smell something wonderful. I eyed the plate intensely with every inch of foil I unfolded. I was paralyzed with pleasure. I knew this plate instantly. I recognized the dressing immediately – the thick cornbread textured stuffing with green peppers, celery and giblets shredded throughout, where every forkful would be garnished with the perfect amount of meat, vegetables and bread. It was my mother's dressing. I could tell that from seeing how it sat on the plate next to my favorite part of the turkey – the wing – with a medium thick slice of old-fashioned ham, macaroni and cheese, greens and Hawaiian sweet potatoes.

I just stared – not eating anything. I was in the mystic zone of dreaming and just didn't want to do anything to spoil the moment. I'd somehow conjured up my favorite meal in all my lifetime and like so many dreams I'd spoiled it by touching things or tasting them and getting so excited I jarred myself awake. I stayed frozen, refusing to spoil the dream. But my eyes kept wandering to the potato salad. It looked just like Mama's with sprinkles of paprika and a generous portion of boiled eggs (her holiday special had extra eggs). I had to taste it; I'd give anything to taste my mother's potato salad again. Even if it was just in a dream and since I knew how they worked, I would wake up the minute the fork reached my mouth. I thought I'd dare not chance it. I stared at the plate for so long that it became evident I was not dreaming – about the plate at least.

I realized I had mingled my Thanksgiving memories of missing Mama into an intense scenario and that I may have been losing my mind. But I was starving and I haphazardly picked a forkful of salad up and shoved it into my mouth. It was heaven; I rushed to cram a couple more mouthfuls in before I awoke. The flavor was unmistakably my mother's. I couldn't believe the dream was still lasting so I spooned up some dressing, my next favorite. I hurried and ate some macaroni and cheese and hadn't woke up yet. I was playing beat the clock eating all these delicious foods until I realized I didn't have to rush – the food was real.

A person knows their mother's cooking. Without question this was my mother's cornbread dressing with Pepperidge Farm Stuffing Mix and oysters. I know the thickness of Mama's Hawaiian sweet potatoes with their rich buttery cinnamon, nutmeg and vanilla blended to perfection and golden toasty marshmallows on top. I know exactly how they stand up on a fork. I know her greens. I don't know how she does them but they were always the signature piece of our holiday meals with ham hocks cooked completely off the bones. Both the skin and the lean meat mingling richly among the greens with their special seasoned pot liquor. But more than anything I know my mother's potato salad and baked ham with its brown sugar and ginger ale glaze, basted over pineapples, cherries and cloves.

That meal was the best Thanksgiving dinner I'd had since my last Thanksgiving meal at Mama's with my family. I was so overjoyed that my depression lifted and I straightened up inside and around my house. I didn't feel homeless or like the derelict I was – living on the sidewalk in downtown Los Angeles.

As night came I decided to go back in and eat the last food I had saved. This time I ate slowly savoring every morsel until it was all gone. I dozed off thinking about the wonderful meal and how nice it would have been to have a big slice of sweet potato pie for dessert. I fell into a comfortable sleep. I awoke to a light tapping on my box. I was super full and a lot lazy from the yard work and the fantastic meal I'd eaten, so I didn't answer.

I heard a familiar voice say, "She must be asleep or not home, so just leave it on the crate for her."

I jumped, completely awoke at the sound of my mother's voice, and stumbled and fumbled to get out of my box to see her. But when I did get out, no one was there. I looked up and down the street but there was no movement anywhere. All I saw was a generous slice of sweet potato pie wrapped in clear plastic and sitting on the milk crate next to my box. I didn't need to taste it to know who it was from. Tears fell freely from my eyes as I lifted my face to the heavens.

"Thank you, Mama. I miss you so much, but this is the best Thanksgiving I've had since you been gone."

Chimara P. Swift

Without A Song
(NOVEL EXCERPT)

It was April 15th, the last day to file income tax. I remember because the traffic on Central Avenue near Gage was tremendously hectic with horns blowing and impatient drivers gridlocked in multiple lanes trying to get to the Post Office.

The noise level was so high I had to holler at the operator just to be heard over the pay phone I was using. She was having trouble placing my collect call home and I was growing impatient with the delay. Between the heavy traffic and my anxiousness to know how Mama was doing, I was starting to get upset. Mama was in the hospital for the umpteenth time with a heart condition she seemed to have developed during the heat wave that hit Chicago that previous summer. I had never known her to be seriously sick, so this continuous illness had me seriously concerned.

In the past, Mama always was strong as a bull. Her friends, who knew her from back in the day, would joke about her having her babies early in the morning so she could get up and put her beans on. She would always take care of herself with home remedies: Watkins products, goose grease, Lilly E. Pinkin, castor oil and stuff like that. But since the heat wave her health seemed to deteriorate to the point where she had to have her foot amputated. Her diabetes and everything else was raging out of control. I was worried and unable to start my day without knowing she was ok.

Because of the tax deadline, money on the streets was good. Motorists stalled in traffic were paying street hustlers to run and get cold beers, cigarettes and sandwiches because they didn't want to lose their place in the lines that were literally taking hours to get into the Post Office parking lot. It was a warm and sunny day in Los Angeles and people were out in droves gallivanting up and down the street. The dope dealers were thick on the corners; the hoes were whoring and the tricks were trickin' off right there in their cars in the middle of Central Avenue. It was wild! The kind of day street people love. The music was loud and rockin'; lots of bull shitting and banter, and the cash was sure to flow until midnight – the cutoff time for filing taxes. I wanted to get in the traffic myself, but I need to check on Mama first.

I thought I heard a familiar voice, so I placed a finger in my free ear to help drown out the background noise. It was my sister.

"How is she," I asked, dismissing formality and greetings cause conversation would just be too hard to have under the circumstances, and I just wanted to get the daily report. I had hit a lick but I had him on hold while I made the call. I needed to turn some corners, check some traps, catch up with some people that knew me or owned me, sling my thing and all of that, which was a lot to put on a business card, so I had to be out there in person.

When I was home in Chicago, around my family I always kept my decadent behavior at a distance from my family and tried hard not to let it be more important than family stuff. It was one of the few values I tried not to compromise because it was one of the few things that made me feel human – family and church. The few years I'd spent totally disconnected – no letters, no calls, no visits – was during a period when I had totally given up on life. I was dead, just not buried. My "now I lay me down to sleep" had become "I hope I never wake from sleep." And every day I wake up to the hell my life had become, my soul would cry in response to the perpetual darkness I dwelt in. That was the sum of my day and night.

My life was like that for a couple of years, until my mother somehow persuaded my brother Rommey to come to California and find me. I don't know how he did it, but I remember leaving McArthur Park early one morning, heading toward my cheap hotel room, when I spotted him. At first I thought I was hallucinating or imagining things, but as I got closer and realized it was Rommey, my heart instantly healed from the joy that I felt, and I never allowed homesickness, depression or my situation to separate me from my family again.

So I had started calling home more frequently, especially since Mama had been sick. I don't know how much time had passed before I realized that someone on the other end was calling my name. It was my sister. Again she was trying to get me to answer her, "Pam. Pam! Are you there?"

I snapped back to the moment. "Yeah, how is she?" I asked again, feeling my voice was being drowned out by the noise and the more than 2,000 miles that distanced us, as were the many many years since I'd left home—estranged and living poorly on the streets of California.

I couldn't hear anything except my regrets for not being there when I should be.

When I went to California years before, I only planned to be there a few months and get back home before my baby was born. I was four months pregnant at the time and on a serious mission.

This was my second pregnancy in ten years. The first one hadn't gone well because in Illinois, at that time, you couldn't put the baby's father's name on the birth certificate unless you were married. If you weren't married, you had to have his—the father's—written consent.

When I told Jimmy Jordan I was pregnant by him, he twisted my arm, almost breaking it off and forced me to say out loud in front of everyone who was present that the baby wasn't his. So that space on my daughter's birth certificate remains blank to this day.

So ten years later when I became pregnant by LeVar Burton and he tells me the baby is not his, hangs up on me, and refuses to accept any more calls from me, the only choice I had was to go out to California and confront him. I realized I was in the same situation again, only this time I wasn't going to accept the bullshit!

The look on Mama's face almost stopped me from going, as she begged me not to go. But I had to. Already people I knew were saying things like "she claims she's pregnant by LeVar Burton, the actor" and "mama's baby, daddy's maybe." I wasn't going to have another child of mine grow up under that kind of accusation and doubt as to who the father was. Plus, I was fighting mad at how LeVar and his manager, Dolores Robertson, were treating me.

So here I was, years later, stuck in California, homeless and strung out on drugs.

"Pam! Pam! Are you there?"

"Yeah. I can hear you now," I said. It was as if the whole world fell silent as I clearly and distinctly hear my sister say, "Mama's gone. She passed away at 10:53 this morning."

I couldn't move – not my mouth nor my hand which was squeezing the receiver so tightly sweat ran down my arm to my elbow. I couldn't move my mind to the next thought which was "WHAT?"

My sister hadn't hung up either. She was waiting for me to answer her, but I couldn't speak. I could hear her telling me they'd make all the arrangements for me to come home, all I needed to do was get to the airport.

"I can't," I said from nowhere. "I can't think that far. I can't move that far. I won't be able to do that," I told her point-blankly. "It's too much for me to do," I said, interrupting her while she was still talking about what flight I needed to take to O'Hare to get there in time for the funeral.

Even though it was a bright warm California day, the sky suddenly opened up and a heavy rain poured down from the sky. For days I was in a daze, unable to do anything. My mind was stuck on the fact that I would never hear Mama's joyful laughter, or her warnings or her wise advice. I will never see her smile again, eat her cooking or get a birthday card with a much needed five or ten dollars in it. And I will never hear her sing again.

From these memories I begin to hum and sing some of the old church songs she had taught me. Before I knew what was happening, I'd gathered up my toothbrush, combed my hair and tossed a dress into an overnight bag and was headed toward LAX.

I hummed and wrote these words as I traveled to Chicago for Mama's funeral. It was our last duet because I could feel something beyond myself helping me get

Chimara P. Swift

there. It was in the song, the melody, the memories and the love I have for my beloved Mama,

> It's been a good life, a long long road
> We've seen mountains and valleys blow
> Kissed the morning sun.
> I've heard you crying in the evening rain.
> But in every storm I've been through
> You were there to lift me up
> Sometimes you'd carry me through
> Mama I love you, want to be with you one day
> Face to face
> It's been a good life
> Although we argued, sometime we'd fight
> With our battles won
> We'd sit together watching the Sun go down
> Singing in perfect harmony
> Cause I'm a part of you
> And you're a part of me
> You make the music
> I just sing along
> I want to hear you say, "I fought the good fight"
> When I run my course and finish my race
> I love you and I just want to rest in your arms
> Know that every breath I take
> Every step I make
> Will lead me home.

That's All She Wrote

On Sneaking Around

Every shut eye ain't sleep, every goodbye ain't gone

On Bad Relationships

You taking your ducks to a muddy pond

On Breaking Up

Get further, smell better

Chimara P. Swift

ABOUT THE AUTHOR: **Chimara P. Swift**

I was born in Chicago in 1952. I am my mother's fifteenth child. I grew up in Englewood and attended Parker Elementary, Simeon Vocational and Kennedy-King College, where I got my Associates degree. I went on to get my BA at Chicago State University. I took some classes in creative writing at Columbia College when it was near the 'S' curve, and I took a few classes at the Art Institute of Chicago and later studied Writing for Film and Television at UCLA.

I always knew I wanted to be a writer. When I would tell people, they would either laugh or tell me that Negroes weren't writers. Seeing the hurt look on my face, they would compromise and tell me I was a smart girl and could easily get a good job. So while I stopped 'saying' I wanted to be a writer, I never stopped 'thinking' about being a writer.

I was in for the surprise of my life when I tried to register at Loop Jr. College and was told my English score was too low for me to be accepted. I had to take English 98, 99 and 100 before I could start Jr. College. I was told my spelling was atrocious and my grammar was juvenile. How did that happen when I'd been in school for 12 years? Nobody had bothered to teach or correct me in an education system that was based on a serious curve, where I had been told I was a good student.

I was pissed. This was worse than walking around smiling all day with collard greens stuck between your teeth and nobody telling you. I was almost illiterate, and I was so embarrassed and ashamed that it was years before I picked up a pen to write anything again.

So, here I am, 67 years of age, and I am just going to go for it. I never gave up writing even though I kept it a secret and never showed it to anybody. But I do believe I have a gift for storytelling and writing songs. I have been working on a musical play titled *Crackin' Up* for the past seven years, and I have been journaling my life story for longer than that. *Without A Song* comes from those journals. I am also putting together several collections of poems I have written over the years.

In my stories I write about a lot of stuff people don't like to talk about: mental illness, drug addiction, imprisonment and abandonment – these are the roads my life took me down. My stories are also full of love and hope for a better tomorrow. The bottom line in life is no matter what you have been through, there is always hope.

I thank God for this opportunity to share these pieces of my life with you.

www.ingramcontent.com/pod-product-compliance
Lightning Source LLC
Chambersburg PA
CBHW070856050426
42453CB00012B/2234